Places Male and Female

11/30/10

With love and happiness!

Places Male and Female

Poems by Jody Helfand

Copyright ©2010 by Jody Helfand. All rights reserved.
No part of this book may be reproduced, stored in a retrieval system, or transmitted in any form or by any means, electronic, mechanical, photocopying, recording, or otherwise, except as may be expressly permitted by the applicable copyright or in writing by the author.
Printed in the United States of America 2010. First Edition.

Cover Art: "Shadows" by Mrutyunjaya Dash
http://fineartamerica.com/featured/bonita-mrutyunjaya-dash.html
Copyright ©2010 by Mrutyunjaya Dash

Cover Layout: Michal Mahgerefteh

Publisher:
Poetica Publishing Company
www.poeticapublishing.com

5.5" x 8.5"   116 ppb
ISBN 978-0-9827958-7-3

Order information:
www.poeticamagazine.com
P.O. Box 11014
Norfolk, VA 23517

$15.00

For

the people who love me

and for Kim Vaeth, who encouraged me.

.

Contents

At The Gynecologist's Office

I. There Is A Boy Somewhere In This Picture

The Nature Of Insects *3*

Her Taste *4*

The Day I Almost Lost Myself *5*

The Teasing *6*

There Is A Boy Somewhere In This Picture *7*

The Boy Girl Game *12*

Twelve And Bleeding *13*

The Pointer Sisters And A Chicken *14*

The Girl In The Boy's Dressing Room *15*

I Feared Her Age The Same Way I Feared Sleep *16*

East Hampton, 1985 *17*

At The Roller Rink *18*

What Comes With An Attraction Between Cousins *19*

Ms. Pac Man In The Afternoon *20*

Fourteen *22*

What We Carried *23*

An Experiment (With A Boy Named Matt) *24*

Under The Moon *25*

II. Places Male And Female

Photo: Girl Lies On The Sand   29

How A Body Survives   32

The Familiar Part Of Sex   33

When I Cut My Hair   34

The Talking   36

A Female Body Hides   37

The Mind's Convincing Tricks   38

Horror Movie   39

My Research   40

A Decision   41

Waiting To Be Without Breasts   42

In The Dark   43

Lines From A Villanelle   45

Terrible Things   46

This Body   47

Two Hormones   48

The Answer   49

Haystack Rock, 1993   50

At The Hospital   51

When A Place Begins   53

An Extension Of   54

The Female   55

I Remember A Time   56

The Poem Is Written On The Body 58

What Makes A Man 59

Places Male And Female 61

Live As A Boy 62

Photos: Man Stands Three Times In Sydney 63

III. Bloodlines

Among The Stones Of Fire 67

Matchmaker 68

Photo: Elderly Jew, Young Boy 69

Mathematician 70

I Pray Near Honeybees 72

The Badger 73

The Seizure 74

The Day We Put My Dog To Sleep 75

Echoes 77

My Father's Hands 78

Wellwood Cemetery, Pinelawn, 1998 80

Your Nature 82

Dark Persistent Blue 83

For You 84

The Red 85

Your Image In Watercolor 86

We Have Sex   *87*

Bloodline   *88*

Danny And The Pink Princess Phone   *89*

What We Heard   *91*

Where Bodies Don't Exist   *92*

The Way We Endured   *93*

Acknowledgments

About the Author

And then the man--?

                    Ah, that's the thing.
Two black deer beside the spring.
The woman first, and when she died,
the man was there. The man inside.

                                  --Martha Collins
                                  "Her Rage"

At The Gynecologist's Office

You don't remember being born. But you were, you came out of a uterus, you did, and then through the canal, the umbilical cord, the cutting, the holding, the crying. Then, the name on the birth certificate, the *male* or *female*. This is what you think about when you sit with the other women who stare at you when your name is called and you walk to the nurse, with your facial hair and your muscles and your deep voice that say *thanks*. Then you sit in the chair while the same nurse from earlier takes your blood pressure and your pulse and tells you it's normal and pretends not to notice that you don't look like a woman. And she laughs and you laugh and you follow her to the room, take off your clothes after she leaves, unfold the paper gown and put it on backwards because you don't really know how to put the paper gown on anyway. And there's a knock at the door and a voice that says, *It's the doctor, can I come in?* And you say *yes* and she says *Oh, you have that on backwards* and you say *oh, thanks, okay,* and she leaves and you leave the paper gown on the way it is and sit and wait for the doctor to come back and read an article about Renee Zellweger in People Magazine. But you can't concentrate because you have to pee and you don't want to leave the room because the other patients will see you. But the thought of something shoved inside there scraping and smearing while your bladder is full is worse, so you open the door, peek your head out, see the doctor, call her and ask where the bathroom is. She points, says *You can use the special bathroom, the one in the back, the one we use,* and offers to walk there with you, but you shake your head and say *no, that's okay, that's alright, I can go by myself, but thanks,* and then walk to the special bathroom in your paper gown, that's hard to find, that's in the back of the office, alone, and squat over the toilet and notice the wallpaper that's pink; it reminds you of cotton candy or flowers in the springtime, and then you finish and wash your hands, and walk back to the room. Nobody sees you. It's a miracle. You've become invisible. And you almost think this won't be so bad, this won't hurt that much, until the doctor knocks again and you say *come in,* and she smiles and tells you to scoot to the end, to spread your legs, to relax, and to breathe, breathe, breathe.

I. There Is A Boy Somewhere In This Picture

The Nature of Insects

Snared by elementary rules,
friends accepted their interests,
hopscotch, tea parties, dress up--
when I wanted to be Captain America.
I studied my ant farm, lost in the calm
of their design. I followed them
through tunnels of exact purpose
and sensed a feeling of bodies
working together to form an industry.
I understood these wingless insects
in their socialized condition.
At night, I told Mr. Lion which girls I liked--
Grrrirls don't marry Girls,
he whispered, as I slept with lips
pressed against a groove in my knuckle,
telling myself Mr. Lion was wrong,
as my ants continued to build their colonies.

Her Taste

Jeannie said
I'm not allowed to play with Jews
She looked like a poodle
her hair curled in light shades

I sat on a swing
in the playground
I'm not Jewish   I said

She gripped the braided metal
and pushed higher
until I jumped
landing in the sand

She fell on top of me
our faces close as our breath
and took my hand in hers

Will you marry me

Yes   I said
kissing her cheek   her
sweat falling like sugar
off my lips

The Day I Almost Lost Myself

In Valley Stream,
an area drained by the expressway,
I almost drowned in my aunt's pool.
The deep end called me, and like a warrior falls
I jumped, discarding the water wings my mother told me to wear.
My weight was an anchor that sank to the bottom.
Bubbles came from my nose and I watched them surface—
I was on the other side of living, and became flat
arms extended like a holy man and welcomed the water.
It moved between my ears, came before me and presented itself
coating my body with polished hands, asking me to stay
wishing me down—
I'd be the ocean, it said.
Everyone starts somewhere, it said.
I wanted to make it mine—turn to liquid and swallow the elixir.
Then I was taken, palms on my waist, and lifted to Heaven.
Everyone stood around deciding on a hot dog or a hamburger,
like there was something spectacular happening under that lid.
But my uncle paid attention,
as if his purpose that day was to take me from safety—
that place I wanted to lose myself in.

The Teasing

The girls make fun of me.
I'm too tall.
My hair is too short; my arms are too thick.

They say: *You act like a boy.*
Why do you act like a boy?

When they come around me at recess
I think   *Silence.*

I leave my body
and become the fence in the background.

I see them yell at something that is empty.
And in the stillness, I define their surroundings.

I am a chemical reaction giving off heat;
a series of rearranged atoms
the absence of sound allows.

There Is A Boy Somewhere In This Picture

1. Photo: Spring, 1979 Rockville Centre

I wear a blue jacket
and stand on the grass with three friends:
April, Sandy, and Linda.

Linda and Sandy crouch down for the picture
their bodies uneven, bent.
Blonde hair covers Linda's right eye and part of her lip.

April holds a present under her arm wrapped in red paper,
her brown hair parted in the middle
where she pressed the comb hours ago.

A white fence two inches tall protects the tulips.

We smile, our shadow vertical on the lawn.
Three windows reflect the house across the street
where tree branches and power lines intersect with the sky.
The reflection is the same white as the Tudor behind us.

Two weather lamps hang on each side of the wooden door,
a stained glass window the shape of a diamond rests in the center.

There is a boy somewhere in this picture.

Linda's arm is around me, her hand on my shoulder, fingers in my fist.
We wear pants. Hers are rolled up.
Mine rest on tan shoes unfolding, unbound.

2. Party

It's my seventh birthday at the pizza parlor.
The booths are the color of clover, the walls brown
with black crisscross patterns. Linda wears a shiny
blue and green jacket. April wears corduroy;
they sit at a table, elbows touching, cheese slices
on white plates behind them. The adults talk.
Every other word is Israel. One says *700
gravestones vandalized on Staten Island.*
Another says: *At least Sadat signed the treaty.*
My mother asks if anyone needs a refill.
The jukebox in the corner plays Led Zeppelin.
Livin', lovin', she's just a woman.
Dough is tossed and a hand moves in circles;
flour falls on a cheek, white specs on a lip.
I play pinball, my body moving with the machine.

3. Autumn

The grey cat meows.
My mother fills a bowl with milk and says: *Take this to the cat.*
After, a scratch runs from wrist to shoulder.

It's fall, the leaves exist in spaces of red and yellow.
I rake them into a pile and jump.
It's safe where it smells of earth.

The blonde twins ring the bell: David and Michael.
I play with them because I want to see their sister Linda
who's three years older than me. There's a black stallion horse
she wants; its tail sticks out of the toy bin.
We trade for a quarter and her Smurf drinking glass.

David and Michael are Batman and Robin, and I am the hostage
of an imaginary Joker, my hands tied to a tree trunk.
There's pain in my wrist as a squirrel disrupts the leaves;
it's the only sound I hear until they untie me.

4. House: Winter

Linda is my babysitter; she tucks me in. I want her to sleep with me.
I count stuffed animals. They outline my body, each has a name.
The swing in the Weeble Wobble Treehouse moves back and forth.
It's the wind.

Bacon fries in the kitchen. Nine plates on the counter are lined
with paper towels to absorb the grease. There are three of us.
I sit at the table in pajamas, hair messy, still in a ponytail
from the night before, and wait to be served.

Gilligan's Island is on in the den.
A quilt is draped over a rocking chair.
I lie on the floor, turn the television to mute during commercials.
The professor flirts with Ginger; I wonder why she's not pregnant.

The dog rolls over near the fireplace. My grandmother sees me
pet the fur below her stomach and says *Don't ever touch her there.*
I do anyway. There are two green couches, a coffee table.
Norman Rockwell in the china cabinet.

Inside this house, behind the window there's a room
where my mother stands half naked with a watering can,
dampening the dry soil. I walk in, turn on the light.
She yells at me to turn it off.
The mole on her right breast shakes,
the plants breathe heavily in the heat.

Adjacent, my father's study; papers on the floor, an old lamp
on the desk. Huge oaks line the icy sidewalk.
A picture of Harry Chapin at his house in Huntington--
The frame hangs next to a leather belt.

5. Spring, 1980

I wear a white outfit
with wrinkles from running around in the yard.
My mother yells out the window: *You'll stain your pants.*
I fall like a catcher, knees in the dirt.

The sun lights my hair, a slow whisper
that gives off golden tones.
Bangs are brushed to eyebrows, earrings in the ears, a ring on my pinky.

Presents are given. Five Star Wars figures, a Superman comic
a bike without training wheels parked in the garage and:
Baskin Robbins for me, and five of my favorite friends.

Two weather lamps hang on each side of the wooden door,
a stained glass window the shape of a diamond rests in the center.

We discuss flavors. Chocolate chip, bubble gum, pralines and cream,
argue about liking and not liking vanilla and
decide on clown cones and flying saucers.

In the car, the windows are rolled down. We wait for my mother.
I say: *Be careful or you'll stain your pants!*
Everyone laughs.

There is a boy somewhere in this picture.

The Boy Girl Game

I'm a boy with my cousin
she's the only one
who lets me do this

We play in her room
use pillows to kiss
kissing is like this with us;
(would it be so bad
 without pillows)
I want to find out

I wear Jim Morrison t-shirts
spend my allowance on baseball cards
and wish every night

that when I wake
I'll be looking down at a boy's body
instead of mine

which reminds me of how
I hate morning
when I can see myself;

how I like the dark
where I don't have to be she
when I pray
to whoever it is
eleven year olds pray to
that when I wake, I'll wake as a boy

Twelve And Bleeding

I was in the shower when it came,
light pink, like the watermelon Starburst I sucked on during recess.
My inner thigh was flat and hairless,
a perfect surface for the blood to seep.
I watched it highlight my skin, giving it a glossy and finished look.
My mother's knock was a noise
that stole me from the blood's display.

You want peanut butter and jelly for lunch?
Her voice was thin through the door.
Are you ok? She asked, knocking harder,
her fist becoming a rock and banging.
For a moment, my body became this noise
misplaced and loud in the voiceless water.
Then she was there, pulling the curtain aside
shaking my shoulders: I thought you slipped and broke your neck.
I started my period, I said, closing my legs.

My mother smiled. It was a proud smile, a knowing smile.
I thought of Eric and Ralph and their bodies
sealed off from this kind of mess.
I wanted to be finished with this blood,
capture it in a bottle and dispose of it in the ocean.
Watch it mix with blue and disappear
away from this house, away from this body.

The Pointer Sisters And A Chicken

As she waited in traffic
my father stomped around the kitchen.
Where is she? How do I cook this?
I stood at the counter, my elbow on the chicken
and touched the pimpled skin; I wanted to bite its thighs.
I dunno, I said, to the space he stood seconds ago.
Now he was at the front door
following the sound of my mother's keys.
They came rushing at each other like snakes.
Where's dinner? We have front row seats. We're late, my father spat.
Then, like an actor taking his dramatic moment
my father lifted the chicken over his head and threw it,
the bird a pink blur disappearing into the living room.
My mother went upstairs and came back with three tickets:
I'm so excited, she cried as she grabbed my arm
explaining the money we'd see later after Burger King
while my father stayed home without his keys.

The Girl In The Boy's Dressing Room

When my grandmother and I shopped for clothes, we went
to the boy's section and looked through racks of dress shirts
and ties, until a salesman came over and told us where the girl's
department was. I let my grandmother handle this: Young man,
she would say, my granddaughter feels comfortable wearing boy's
clothing. Will you please help us find her size? Then, arms filled
with clothes, I went to the boy's dressing room as my grandmother
kept searching for other styles that would fit me. As she did this,
I was aware of the salesman standing outside my dressing room,
switching from one foot to the other, describing pretty dresses—
trying to take the girl out of the boy's dressing room.

I Feared Her Age The Same Way I Feared Sleep

Eating cereal reminds me of my grandmother,
her chapped lips touching the spoon
the wrinkles on her throat moving,
as she swallowed milk and bran and dates.
I'd sit across from her peeling hard-boiled eggs,
the shells settling in my dish.
She'd ask about school, told me math was useless
and condemned the kids who teased me to hell,
then refilled my apple juice.
She was a masculine girl who ran with the boys—
everyone said she'd never marry.
She warned me about having too many muscles,
showing me the loose skin underneath her triceps.
At night she'd tuck me in,
touching my arms with wrinkled hands,
and I'd lie there, fearing her age the same way I feared sleep;
my body snug and sealed under the covers.

East Hampton, 1985

We took a walk, away from my house
left the adults to barbecue the steak, chicken, corn.
The sun followed us
until we reached a grove of elms and
then it left; it wasn't welcome here
where the trees touched
reaching their branches out
to meet others like themselves.

We held hands, the way cousins do
our sneakers slid on the dirt road
until we stopped and she let my hand go.
I'm tired, she said and kneeled under a thick branch.
I sat, knees touching the floor, feet tucked under my legs.
Do you have a boyfriend yet? she asked, her arm touching mine.
I studied her lips, full and pink, the mole on her nose.
Justin, I said, *But it's not serious.*

I noticed the sun then, peaking through the leaves
a place the shade overlooked.
I didn't want to move. I wanted her arm to touch mine forever.
I'm dating two boys. Ronnie and Jeffrey. Ronnie gave me this ring.
Her skin pressed against mine as I pulled at the grass.
It was smooth and narrow and
pushed itself between my fingers, then fell
uprooted and unprotected, onto the earth.

At The Roller Rink

It's Friday night. My parachute pants swoosh
as I skate across the carpet past the Asteroids machine,
toward Nancy who leans against the railing
and eats popcorn out of a red basket.
Her jeans are tight, and pink leg warmers hug her calves.
Hi, she says, the freckles on her face moist with sweat.
Hi, I say, and stop, pressing my toe to the floor.
I'm here with Pete, who are you with?
I point to a boy I don't know. *Oh, he's so cute*, she says.
I feather my hair with a comb from my back pocket, run my hands
down the left and right sides of the feathers to make sure they're even.
From the corner I hear: *Happy birthday to you.*
Happy birthday dear Joey, happy birthday to you.
A boy blows out candles, a chocolate cake and a stack of presents next to him.
Blue lights flash in circles on the ceiling and disco balls shine,
as a voice says, *Couples only now. Couples only on the floor.*
I want to hold Nancy's hand, my laces glowing in the dark,
put my arms around her waist, lead her through the shadows.
Instead, I mouth words: *Heard it from a friend who, heard it from a friend who,*
heard it from another you've been messing around.
I hold a make-believe microphone and Nancy laughs. Wanna skate? I ask.
That's gross, she says. Yeah, that's gross, I say and reach for some popcorn,
waiting for the song to end so I can cross one leg over the other
and drop my body fast around the corners. And into the shadows.

What Comes With An Attraction Between Cousins

It's not a side dish, like coleslaw.
It's a feeling of eating the whole pastrami sandwich
and licking the rye seeds off your plate—
That's what I wanted to do to her.
I'd wear my best jeans and pull shirts on and off
until I found one she'd like.
In the car my walkman played slow songs:
Total Eclipse of The Heart, and I'd imagine us
her arms falling as water does
around my neck.
When my father rang the bell
I'd stand like I wasn't concerned
looking at the paint on her door
or the woods by her house.
She'd come to me, socks sliding
black hair I'd smell later.
I wanted to be scratched by her nails—
red letters drawn up and down my arms.
When I said hello, she'd kiss my cheek
and I waited for those moments
re-living her lips on my skin.
We'd go to her room like we were holding
an important business meeting.
I'd tell her my idea for the night:
This time I'll be a cowboy you arrested
and with a pillow between our faces
we kissed until it was time to go—
her hands a tremble away from missing.

Ms. Pac Man In The Afternoon

At the arcade, boys gathered in swarms:
I can beat her! I can beat her!
As if the only thing they knew how to do
was talk in exclamation points around me.

I'd keep myself quiet,
my thumb sweating with the joystick,
until I was cornered by the red and aqua ghosts--
the slightest touch of their body to mine, finishing me.

I played for points,
waiting close to the pie, teasing..... I'd eat it..... 200.....
following its eyes back to the box--
And just as the ghost formed, I'd go through it and survive.

There'd be great noise and excitement,
a hullabaloo, as boys put their quarters on the machine
to guarantee a turn, and I finished the dots,
ready for the next stage.

Then a bonus scene: An intermission.

Pac Man chasing me-- back and forth
with carnival music, and finally, our baby, Junior--

The image of sex a simple explanation for the innocence that played.

The next level was always too much for me,
the banana hopping around
the ghosts hardly staying blue after I ate the pie,
and I'd retire, my body tired from a busy day.

The boys shot their single *Ohh!*, like failed men at a ball game
and I'd go home, eager to meet the next afternoon
to see whose initials would be posted,
and whose quarters would be secured to the screen.

Fourteen

I wore high-top sneakers and ripped jeans.
I walked the halls of high school with cigarettes in my back pocket,
my hair long and blonde with natural waves.
The boys in the courtyard who smoked with me
offered thin joints if I'd make out with them behind the stairwell,
but I didn't do boys.
Dawn met me each morning before homeroom;
she'd smile and ask if we were watching a movie later.
I'd say: Yeah, a horror movie, come over at eight.
After school, I'd sit in the back of the bus with Jesse.
Wanna go to the park tonight, I got some sweet hash?
his voice yellow, like his eyes, his face scarred from picking his acne.
I'd take my breasts and squeeze them together.
Why? So you can touch these, I'd ask, and seize his neck.

At home I'd make pizza bagels and figure out science
then flip my hair upside down and back again to heavy metal,
until the doorbell rang and I looked out the window
to see Dawn holding a bottle of Mountain Dew.
We'd go in the den and sit on the couch.
She'd cross her legs and I'd spread mine,
her shirt cropping up to reveal her bellybutton.
I'd press play with a bowl of popcorn on my lap,
our fingers touching around each kernel
then moving away to our mouths.
I'd watch her lick the salt off her lips with her tongue
as someone painted murals in my stomach
and I grabbed her hand as a girl screamed—
our bodies the weight of flowers curling into each other.

What We Carried

I don't remember when they grew;
one day they were there, ripe and hanging
off my chest. I pressed on the nipples
with my thumbs and pushed them in
as far as they would push; cupped a breast
in my hand and brought it to my mouth.
When I was fourteen, they were still not part of me
as I lay on a mildewed cot in Steven Mannelli's garage.
He said: *I expected more,* then stood in a section of light
between the shadows and pulled his pants down.
It was calm and wilted and I thought
if it could walk, it would walk with difficulty.
Then I reached for it and pinched the tip
with my fingers. It was compliant; always suspended
always carried around. It was also ugly
its veins pressing against the surface
stretching the skin, trying for the outside.

An Experiment
(With A Boy Named Matt)

When I was fifteen, I went with a boy named Matt.
I was a masculine girl and he was effeminate—
slim and tall with sandy brown hair that lay flat,
the lines from his comb still visible in the morning.
After school we'd study algebra equations,
each letter representing a number I didn't understand.
His sister sat with us and smiled at me
the silver of her braces
gleaming with the strokes of sun
coming in through the window.
Sometimes his mother came home with bags of groceries.
I'd carry the heavy ones, my arms full of brown paper
that crinkled on the kitchen counter.
Matt helped us unpack, his slender fingers
gripping heads of lettuce and gallons of milk.

One night, a storm hit, wetting the roof with force.
I watched as drips of water covered the windows
and felt my stomach rouse
when his mother said I should stay over.
I slept in his sister's room with the rain tapping;
the two of us side by side.
I waited until the house was quiet
then crept into Matt's bed.
I placed my hand underneath his boxers
and felt him stiffen as I kissed him,
my tongue rubbing against his teeth.
He touched the muscles in my back as I breathed in his face:
Let's do it, let's have sex.
He stopped, his penis shrinking.
We're too young, he said. Too young to have sex.

Under The Moon

I was in the backyard with my cousin Beth.
I was finishing a bottle of plum wine
and she was smoking by our bonfire
when my mother came out in her bathrobe
holding a bucket of water.
Do you want to set the house on fire?
Her face was staunch: *Do you want to kill us all?*

My response was slow, a drunken reaction,
the wine giving me a sweet calm.
I was biddable, I was numb,
because nothing could top my father's news--
That we were moving to Hawaii.

Beth rose to apologize, her breath hot in the winter air,
as my mother dumped the water over our fire.
You're sixteen. You should know better.
My cousin nodded and slipped her hands
underneath my arms to lift me off the grass.

Her fingers were pale, her knuckles small.
This was the last of her touch,
a savory affection under the fullness of the moon;
its light passing into my eye reflecting her image.

II. Places Male And Female

Photo: Girl Lies On The Sand

1. What Troubles Her

She lies on the sand in her leopard skin bathing suit
with blonde hair everyone says never to cut.
The legs are so tan. She's sideways for the camera
a hand spread on her right thigh
that's smooth from shaving above the knee.
What troubles her is the smile; the teeth
ready to fall out. And the photographer
who can't seem to take his eyes off her.
He says: *That's good, right there. Smile.*
The sand is wet; coarse and damp between
her fingers. It slips into her bathing suit
sticks to the skin and itches. She might as well be naked
she thinks as her palms sweat under the electric sun.
Her cleavage is happening and her gold chain shines
as her mother watches from under a palm tree.

2. Camera Man

The camera is at a strange angle and can't quite capture
this teenage girl; the swimsuit covers too much. *I want to see more*

I need to see more, he thinks, clicking three more times.
Her hair is so blonde, with natural waves and curls. It would feel nice

on his skin, her laying on top. Those lips, so full and apple red
kissing his chest, then moving further down.

A bird circles in the sky; if a picture is taken of this bird, it will rain.
The camera stays focused on the body as the ocean makes sounds;

the waves are not satisfied, they want to be bigger, they want to be
like the ones on The North Shore. They want respect,

but all they do is provide a warm bath for the tourists,
a minor disruption for windsurfers.
They long to be bigger. To curl. They long to be pipeline.

3. Who Is That Girl?

Who is that girl
with green eyes
lying on the sand
as the waves roll in.

Where did the hands come from
so obedient and flat;
it's not natural
this position. It's not natural
but it looks good.

Why is the sky such a blinding
shade of blue
and why is that smile there.

The gold necklace
is laced and thin and
so is the bracelet.

Her forefinger and thumb
form a V as feet touch
on the moist surface.

She leans, her left shoulder
forearm and bicep make
a 90 degree angle. She knows this
from math class and

this is what she thinks about
plus her hand
not so firmly pressed
as the one on her thigh
that leaves no space for air.

How a Body Survives

When I was a lesbian the women I'd date
were careful not to touch me in places female.
I'd tell them I was male,
that I was waiting to change
like female crabs wait
to release their eggs to the sea at midnight
and that I could die in the process—
foam at the mouth
while others ate my leftovers.
It would be a scene,
like thousands of tiny claws trying to reach water
scaling each other to stay alive.
I'd sit on the bed and stare at their questions like
I was looking at the ocean and couldn't see anything
except the immeasurable blue—
the uncertainty of the tide.

The Familiar Part of Sex

She wanted to touch my breasts in the dark.
I said *No, that's not allowed*
and kissed her, keeping my shirt on.
Always, before intimacy, a contract--
to touch my back, arms, and legs only
and never to bother with places female.

My hands ran across her body
and stopped at the curve of her hips.
My tongue rested on her thigh,
arousing the area between my legs
that was forbidden.
She squeezed my arm as her hands
took their place on my back, and said:
Why won't you let me touch you?

This question, the familiar part of sex
and my response kept in memory to repeat each time:
Because I like to please you. That was our agreement, remember?
But I want to please you, too, she said--
Take your jeans off. Let me see your body.

My body, hiding behind clothes and the illusion of male.
A disguise that always lost its skin
in the mirror, in the shower, during sex.

And underneath,
the temporary female who stayed until morning
giving me a link between;
a bridge to walk across
that connected female to male,
and places impossible to understand.

When I Cut My Hair

I grabbed my hair in fistfuls
and pulled until my eyes teared.
Then I was calm, as I walked to the desk drawer
and took out scissors used
for cutting paper or tags off clothes.

I went to the bathroom
holding the scissors
and looked in the mirror at my hair.
It was long and blonde,
its natural color like tones in fall foliage.
It was the last feminine part
of my appearance.

I teased it for a moment,
taking the scissors close
to its golden strands,
close to its natural waves, making it sweat.

The hair was so thick
that I had to press the handles
firmly together for a couple of seconds
before I heard the sound of blades cutting through.

As it fell, it made piles on the floor,
its own messy wig,
and when I looked in the mirror
my face was relieved and a voice
told me to go all the way,
to get a razor and shave it off.

Then, I was looking in the mirror
at my bald head, thinking *How could I do this?*
What will people think?

But those were my mother's words,
not mine, and I looked on the ground again
at the piles of hair, and thought *more of her is gone.*
My hair would grow back.
But more of her was finally gone.

The Talking

At the Chinese restaurant my aunt says,
Oh my God! You're bald! That pretty hair! Why'd you cut off that pretty hair?

If I'm not careful, she says, I'll become my Aunt Iris, who lives alone
in a rent controlled apartment in Manhattan, with so many books
she can't see the floor or find her way to the kitchen.

Don't become her, my cousin says.
Her lips are shining with pink lip gloss.

I am sinking low in my chair,
barely holding a piece of broccoli in my chopsticks.
I've made the terrible mistake of listening.

At the lesbian bar, an acquaintance says,
Where'd your hair go? That hair was so hot woman!
I am bald, like Sinead O'Connor, like Kojak, she says, then walks away.

On the dance floor, she moves very slow to some awful rhythm,
whispers something in her girlfriend's ear, then puts her hands in the air.
Her breasts bounce.
I am as uncomfortable as the sofa in the corner that nobody ever sits on.

On the bus, a little girl points.
Is that a girl? She asks her mother. Or a boy? A girl or a boy?
I hear, *Shhhhhhh, honey. Shhhhhhhhh!*

I am as awkward as something that's been broken
so many times, then fixed, something you just can't throw away yet.
I am a boy, I say. A bald boy.

A Female Body Hides

At a club I am the goth boy goth girls stare at with curiosity.
They sense the outer realm of *femaleness* that orbits.

Through blue smoke some girls watch,
while one walks over in platform heels, her black dress touching the floor.
She says, *I love this song, I love Bauhaus.*

I take her hand, notice silver rings, some with gemstones,
some with crosses, her nails a deep cranberry.
Your eyes are so blue, she says, as we walk to the dance floor.

She doesn't know electrical tape holds my breasts down
and a female body hides underneath my clothes.
I say nothing, and the man she assumes becomes real.

She touches my waist during a slow part of the song,
and I move her hand away.
Mysterious, she says in my ear.

Her breath causes a chill that makes the hair on my arms stand up.
I fake a smile and continue to dance,
my breasts in place, held down, trying not to move.

The Mind's Convincing Tricks

I took a picture of my breasts
and left it on the bathroom sink.
I looked at it every morning
while brushing my teeth, and thought: How can I make these work?

How the mind manipulates.
One day it's *I can keep these,*
it's no big deal, I'm still a man inside.

The next day it's get rid of them, they're red flags.
If you have to, cut them off; use the knife in the kitchen drawer.

Then, one night after reading Derrida
I think the word *breasts* means nothing.
A construct to deconstruct.
Meaningless letters in a poisonous language.

I try to see new meaning in the words *tits,*
jugs, melons, and think I can do this.
I can live as a man with two lumps of fatty tissue on my chest.

But the problem is using language to make sense
of it; trying to think of a new language, a new way to find meaning
in the visual image of breasts in the mirror,
and the mind's convincing tricks.

Horror Movie

My mind is a horror festival tonight.
Zombies are eating brains,
men are turning into werewolves,
vampires are sleeping in their coffins.

There is a murderer in the woods, too.
He wants to strangle someone.
He crunches leaves with his boots.

There is another movie I play.
Waking up during surgery and feeling the scalpel slice through skin.
But there's a catch: The mind is awake.

The body is not, so I can't speak
or open my eyes, but I feel everything,
even the hard callous underneath the surgeon's glove.

Rachmaninoff plays on a small stereo.
I know this one, it's the one I listen to,
the one I can't play because it's too fast.
Then the Finale, The *Alla breve*, that unites.

This is the soundtrack.
And at the end, the four-note rhythm, the signature,
as I feel my left breast come off and then my right.

Every zombie disappears, every werewolf eaten
by vampires, every vampire stabbed in the heart
with wooden crosses, but

the murderer is still out there crunching leaves
with his boots, walking around in the woods,
waiting for the right time to strangle someone.

My Research

The doctors don't know the answers.
They shrug their shoulders,
say I've never had a patient like you,
a female to male trans...

I am an interesting case for their notes.
Something to talk about at lunch.
I need to figure out how to be a success.
An award winner.

There are times I feel like screaming,
like saying *I am a person.*

One doctor wants to study me.
Monitor my liver.
Take pictures of my face, my naked body, my brain.

He wants to know if my thought patterns
will change when I start hormones.
He asks permission, says *It's a good thing to do for others.*

I am my own experiment now,
who says what blood tests I need,
what dose of hormones I want.
They trust me, my false confidence, my *research.*

I say, we need to slow down, go with caution,
as if we're driving in a downpour with our headlights off.

I am terrified because my research is so limited.
I am terrified, because they listen.

A Decision

I realized my spirit
would be cut into pieces and scattered
in the furthest corners.

Finding the pieces was completely up to me,
but a penis would never be found,
because one never existed in the first place.

Like Osiris, one would be made,
but not carved from wood; instead grown by my body,
stuck, before the idea emerged
to deconstruct then reconstruct.

These concepts applied to the body,
but not *my* body anymore.
A new body, but first the female body, torn down.

Not just a remodeling, but a completely new location,
the old rules thrown away,
the new rules not yet thought about.

This wasn't *gender identity disorder*,
I didn't have some kind of sickness.
It was a simple idea.

I had to destroy myself before finding myself.
It was the anguish of being in a place
where all I could see was female.

Waiting To Be Without Breasts

Sometimes waiting was a sunset,
its color a fireworks of desire set aside.
I was oblivious to color.
Sunsets were ugly.

Other times, waiting was a pilgrimage,
there was something to be learned.
I would think, it was time
for their ultimate punishment.
They knew punching.
They knew black and blue.
But they didn't know the scalpel.

Waiting to be without breasts
was like waiting for a total solar eclipse,
the moon passing between earth and sun,
the sun's glowing corona the only light
from a startled sky.

In The Dark

I leave you in the dark.
It's better not knowing
the complications hormones can cause.

It's better not knowing I could die
in surgery because my pulse
may be too slow to handle it.

This isn't what you want.
You say, *Some mothers wouldn't want to know,
but I do, so tell me everything.*

You like to worry about me;
this is how you get comfortable.
Like overeating, worrying is a bad habit
having an only child causes.

You say, *as long as it's safe,
as long as you're happy,
I can call you he. I can think of you as my son now.*

At night you realize your daughter is gone,
as the dogs sleep beside you,
curled up against your body.

You remember the girl
who went into the dressing room with you
and saw you naked.

You think: Did I do something to cause this?
A revolving thought,
a merry-go-round of thought, that makes you question
if you've been a good mother.

You fall asleep thinking of the little girl you put dresses on,
of the grandchildren you thought you'd have.

There are no answers in the dark,
and whether you know it or not,
you like it that way.

Lines From A Villanelle

The sun reminds me of Rachel.
I see her in the market with a guitar
and a tin of lavender hand salve.

It's surreal.
I say: *Pick a pronoun and call me he. I appear and reappear when you say he.*
(Lines from a villanelle she'll use in her next song)

She drifts between aisles
and stops to buy food for her cat Camille;
the one she left out on the roof for six hours during a blizzard.

It's surreal.
She brushes past and says: *Excuse me, I didn't see you in the aisle.*
A slight touch of my arm-- her hand

holds me for a moment, before I see
the woman I shared my body with.
Her hands on my breasts, over my thighs,

the curve of her tongue looking for something more
than the image of me in her bed.
And my words: *I appear and disappear when you say
she,* before I left.

Terrible Things

My father said: You're lucky to have that body. There are people who have all kinds of terrible things on their bodies and those are the ones who should be concerned. Besides, a good surface begins with what's underneath. Layers of soil and mineral; that's what counts. I became a forest then, regulating nutrients and shedding my leaves. I was also the business of tree farming and heard, *Timber Timber* as my trunks and crowns were discarded. My body will be similar. Ovaries, tubes, and breasts taken by doctors who make incisions and label what was once attached, waste.

This Body

When I was sixteen
a nurse slipped a needle under my vein—
It felt like a pushpin pressing into cork.
When the vial was full, she pulled at the needle
like an ingrown hair, and I bit my tongue.
She said: *Press harder on the gauze,*
her neck taken by moles and beauty marks
set to puff and raise.
I remember her as I sit on the sink
with a syringe and touch the tip to my thigh.
I can't push through a place I can't go inside of—
bundles of myofibers and strands of protein.
If I could walk by, inspect the most private area of bone
then I could stick the needle in—watch the tip nest
and pull out to see my blood catch
at the end of the needle and drop
like columns of air in a current—
then I could let the liquid flow to form this body.

Two Hormones

It was hard to find myself.
I was part of each hormone.
One minute my voice was male, and I puffed out my chest
looking to fight anyone who stared.
The next minute *she* came out,
trying to convince him to *just let it go.*

Who to listen to?
I was a bag of stereotypes; I didn't know how to stop myself.
I went through menopause.
Hot flashes. Feeling fat. Crying.
I was on an emotional swing.
The body was tricked, but the mind was not.

The mind knew that while the eggs dried up,
the man was making his way through.
Unpacking his bags, putting his clothes on hangers,
watching the woman move out.

Watching her walk all the way down the stairs
without even a glance over her shoulder,
and then sitting at the kitchen table
saying *You think I'm leaving now? It's just starting to get good.*

They say you shouldn't be in a relationship when this is happening.
You shouldn't talk to your family too much, either.
You'll blow up at the slightest thing.

But for me, the challenge
wasn't getting along with whoever I was dating
or listening to my family question my decision.
The challenge was convincing the woman to leave.
Making her get up from the kitchen table
and walk out the door.

The Answer

I'd been on testosterone a year
my breasts shrinking, my voice lowering.
They hired me as male,
wrote my name in the schedule as *Mr.*

I was an exaggerated macho man
and sniffed my nose like I was important.
My shaved head was an expression, a form of confidence.
I'd intimidate them like an angry parent;
scare them so they wouldn't focus on my body.

Many were in uniform as I stood at the podium:
This is writing 120, I said with plenty of bass, my talk a trance.
These men could lift the heaviest artillery,
their muscles packed and ready to burst.

But in the back, a thin boy sat studying me, and after class he stayed.
You said we can research anything? I research Hitler. That's cool, right?

I thought of my ancestors; if I was trapped
would I pretend to be someone else?
The answer was as awkward as the boy in front of me.
A twisted kind of thinking to save myself.

Haystack Rock, 1993

I went during winter.
It almost snowed on the beach.
The tide was low so I walked to the rock.

I looked at a starfish in one of the tide pools
and thought, I'll be one of the many
who are stranded out here when the tide comes in.

I would do this on purpose so I could be alone,
so I could have it to myself,
without the idea of gender as a distraction.

Is my beard full enough, are my breasts showing?
None of this to interfere in the experience
of this tall monolith.

I remember clearly how the mind distracts.
How it takes away from something so pure,
its agenda to ruin, to spoil an experience
almost impossible to spoil.

At The Hospital

A nurse inserted a needle through my skin
and into my vein. Dextrose, she said.
There were a cluster of moles on her neck
in the shape of a triangle.

Weren't moles in the shape of a triangle
supposed to mean you're special?
I asked her that. She smiled and said
When you wake up, don't make any sudden moves.
Your abdomen will be very sore, very vulnerable.

It was still dark outside.
The shadows said, *don't do this,*
and I thought, always before a trip, the news
about planes crashing.

Always before surgery, shows like 20/20
about people who wake up
in the middle of surgery,
called, *Anaesthesia nightmares.*

My thoughts were obsessive; the needle in my vein
was suddenly sharp, its tip pressing.

The nurses in the hospital were impostors,
schoolteachers and government clerks
who had no idea what they were doing.

The dextrose was poison, killing me slowly.
There was no surgeon; instead, I'd wake up
in a bathtub missing a kidney, my ovaries and breasts
still in place, the estrogen going wild.

On the way to the operating room,
my heart beat fast, the way it did before
an important performance or accepting an award.

I kept thinking about the shadows and their voices,
saying *don't do this.*
Were they real? Or were they an echo of my voice,
afraid of the happiness that peace brings?

When A Place Begins

My body folds like places
beneath and bounded
by moisture that makes the skin
stick to itself.
I've seen how a body can amend
once the decision is made;
a revising, then a shape.
The process is kept like pieces of a past
or secrets between lovers
then shot like a glance
when the knowing comes.

An Extension Of

My mother said that men
are an extension of their size—
that everything's a pissing contest.
When I'm in the men's room
there's no challenge, I go to a stall.
If a man holds himself out, I look through
a small opening to see how he does it
his palm engaged, and fingers curled
like a defunct spider. I've watched a man
investigate like this, careful as an ant
who uses its antennae to taste.
He looks over with the agility of a soldier
then retreats, his neck snapping back to center.
It's his nature to wonder—a need to understand
this organ that makes it dangerous.

The Female

I thought I'd forgotten her.
Strange how we trick ourselves
into forgetting what will never be lost.

She's here, somewhere inside.
A ghost who follows me from house to house.
The female.

But her body is gone.
Like a parallel universe, like a dimension
that may or may not exist.
Her essence, her soul is here.

A magician's magic, everyone believes
when he makes a bunny, a coin, or a body disappear.
She was an illusion, but she was real.

I try to forget, I burn the pictures,
but she won't go away.
She is an old enemy I can't help but respect,
and destroy again if I had the chance.

I Remember A Time

I remember a time when my father said
I don't know what to think of you as,
as we walked to the bathroom, and he went
to the urinal and I went to the stall.
He said, *Wait in the stall until I'm done.*
I was ashamed, quarantined with the graffiti on the wall.

My father didn't know what to think of me as,
because he knew me only as a girl.
My gender confused him.
I was a word problem he couldn't figure out.
He gave up on something he didn't understand,
because the ego was in the corner coaching him.

I remember a time when a lesbian friend
called me *she* in front of the waiter,
even though my beard was thick and curly.
I'm him, I said to the waiter. *He. I don't know why she called me that.*
But I did know why.
I left the women to be with the men, I was a traitor.
One less butch to be auctioned off, one less Drag King.

If I said I was female, I was accepted.
It didn't matter if I looked like a man, if I said *Honey,
get me a beer,* to my girlfriend in the lesbian bar--
That wasn't sexist, that was role playing.
I was their theme park, but if they looked closer,
they'd notice everything was fake.

I remember a time when my girlfriend told me to keep my breasts.
Was she gay, straight, bisexual?
My breasts were a comfort.

How could a lesbian be attracted to a man?
After sex, I told her it was over, that I'd known for weeks.
She said, *You're cruel like a guy.*

I was cruel, she was right.
Taking cues from movies and television.
Behaving the way I thought a man should behave.
I'd been brainwashed like my father, like my friend,
like my girlfriend, and didn't know that one day I'd escape,
run from the cult, the deprogramming taking years,
the recovery questionable.

The Poem Is Written On The Body

I've studied myself as carefully as a poem
printed with and without the comma,
with and without italics,
to see which version reads best.

My body has been revised many times,
letters changed, words scrutinized.
The surprises never stop.

I could wake up tomorrow
with a hairier back and larger feet.
Or a bigger penis,
once the size of an apple seed,
then finding its shape after months of swelling and growth.

I've been told it's still growing,
a mimicry, trying to reenact puberty.

Seeing myself can be as exciting as a trip
that's been planned for years,
and as frightening as the airplane landing
in the middle of a lightning storm.

The poem is written on the body,
and I observe closely, a spectator in the body's field,
aware of its revising.

What Makes A Man

Why is it necessary to have a penis constructed,
made from parts of my skin, made from silicone--
part Frankenstein, stitched together with needles, sewed, taped on,
glued from parts of other parts.
Is a penis what I need to feel complete?

When I'm in the locker room, I think about this.
When I'm in the bathroom, when I'm naked, when I'm felt up
by a security guard at a concert, I think about this.

I've asked myself these questions too many times,
the light bulb blown out, making a clinking sound when it's shaken:
What makes a man?

Thoughts formed while growing up, common ideas
about what body parts belong to what gender?
People expecting me to look a certain way when I'm naked?
The hard division of gender.
The boundaries.

In sports, all the rules, all the penalties, all the practice.
The male and female bathrooms.
The department store categories.
The dolls or cars-- the dollhouses or raceways.

So now the issue?
What to put on my body to match how I feel.
A penis?
Such is magic.
To be tricked, to be suckered out of what I thought to be true,
if it rotted off, if there were complications,
if I lost feeling down there forever.

I already knew the answer before I researched this.
I don't need a penis.
Unless, of course,
there was a way to make it appear suddenly
or to be born again, with one.

Places Male And Female

Female places have become like old ghost towns, once teeming with life,
now abandoned. Undercurrents of female territories slip my mind.

It would be easy to say that all women talk about
is men, makeup, and their bodies. And lesbians-- depending on their age,
talk about feminism, separatism, the politics of butch and femme,
Joan Armatrading, Ani Difranco, strap ons, and cats.

It would be harder to say I don't remember these women,
that I'll never be a tourist giving back life to these old towns,
that it wasn't a plague or an order to leave, it wasn't a lack of resources.
There was a time when gold was all I thought about,
but when the gold was gone, I had to leave.

I moved to male places, where men talk about women,
sex, sports, and their bodies, and gay men-- depending on their age,
talk about sex, Pall Malls, drinking, parties, and Madonna.

In places male, I was still learning, like a child taking cues
from his parents, mimicking their behavior,
until the day he finds out his parents aren't always right.

In female places, I was trained to act, to memorize lines,
to know when to exit.   If I forgot my lines, I was scolded,
but when I didn't wear my costume and refused to exit, I was fired.

Like mining for gold, repetition created false hope.
Shoulders were sore, backs were broken, some almost died,
but most found nothing.

Except the ones who kept at it, their gold close, even in the midst of death
and the idea that one day, they would have to find a new place.

Live As A Boy

I watched the boys run through sprinklers
their bare chests and small nipples moist.
I lived as a boy:

I had my first crush on Nancy, and told my friend
to tell his friend to tell Nancy that I liked her.
I reached the top of the rope in gym class
and didn't have to walk the balance beam
or change with girls in the locker room.
Nobody called me "tomato tits" at recess
and I swung from the monkey bars—
my body right, my timing perfect
to win chicken fights with other boys.
I went swimming in shorts
and didn't have to worry about pads or tampons.
My shoulders grew wide, and I got taller
as girls sat on the bleachers
talking about me and my friends
and how cute we looked playing soccer in the mud.
I picked my date up and met her parents and
put my arm around her during the movie.
We kissed in my car and she moved my hand away.

I watched the boys run through sprinklers
their laughter stainless—
free as water, and just as clear.

Photos: Man Stands Three Times In Sydney

There is a clock in the garden and a man
standing for the camera holding a black leather jacket.
His head is shaved. There is an elephant made of leaves.
Purple and red flowers glow in the light.
The paint is chipping on the railing.

He's not allowed in this garden with the clock and the railing
but he jumps over anyway.
It says: *80 years*, with a *I*, *II*, *III*, and *IV* on its face.
This is how he's supposed to tell time.
The hands are raised a foot off the ground
and he sits on one gigantic piece of metal to pose.

This is the zoo. He smiles for the picture; a giraffe reaches its head
out to the crowd. Everyone's back is turned. Nobody notices him.
Everyone wants the giraffe to touch their fingers, to eat from their hands.

There are two trees. One has green leaves and is tall and sharp;
the other is barren, exposing itself. Its character lies in its emptiness.
And the alarming contrast it creates among the living.

This one looks more familiar, but he is still changing.
Soon the lips will not be as full, the face will be more angular.
There will be more hair under his chin, he will need to buy
a razor and ask his father for advice. His hairline will recede

but this isn't clear; instead, the tight shirts are; the smile is.
He stands on the promenade along Farm Cove at twilight
looking at the poised arch of the Harbour Bridge and
at the Opera House that's under construction
its sail-like roofs almost mystic.

III. Bloodlines

Among The Stones of Fire

> *"... listen to what I am speaking to you;*
> *do not be rebellious like that rebellious house.*
> *Open your mouth and eat what I am giving you."*
>   --Ezekiel 1:8

It was the Jewish Star that reminded me of him
and the bracelet that said: "All my love,
Rose," with the letter B and the numbers 32437058.
He was the only one in the family who went to temple,
who wore a prayer shawl, who strapped on the phylacteries.
My mother says: I don't want to have anything to do with temple--
I've had my share in Malverne.
My mother works on Saturdays and puts birthday candles in the menorah.
She doesn't believe in God, it's an energy from above--
Pray to the energy.
I don't know who's real anymore, the once atheist
turned agnostic turned Buddhist turned reform Jew,
then back to the energy--
The deified cosmos, grandfather of the universe,
who whispers: *Patience is half of wisdom. Don't you see?*
Patience is half of wisdom,
as I read The Torah and The Art of Happiness--
As if happiness and art are a couple holding hands in the park,
moving in the direction of old age, illness, and death,
with a smile on their faces and the knowledge
of just what it takes to discuss the nature of love
in both divine and earthly form--
To be born from the signet of perfection,
full of wisdom, and perfect in beauty.

Matchmaker

They stood in the same tree.
The light wasn't visible
but forty days before they were born
it was decided.

We spend a lifetime looking, don't we?
Another lifetime
if we don't respond.

Their black hair, their eyes far apart
their thin lips.
His shadow not dark behind her.

So, will they bend
like seedlings toward the light
or will they curl
like death, behind us?

Photo: Elderly Jew, Young Boy

Did you know the stings of the nettle
are like hypodermic needles?
My grandson tells me too
that holly leaves have tough spines
and there is a plant that pairs its leaves
to form a moat that can drown a snail.

I sit in this chair and think of him.
Trees surround me.
I hold my walking stick.
Don't be fooled.
The little boy you see in the background
is only my desire for him to be young again.

My grandson is a teacher.
When he talks, he moves his hands.
He tells me about the acacia tree
whose thorns become hollow
when an ant desires sweetness.
He says: Thorns can either be straight

(like on a rose) or they can be curved
which makes them dig in when they are pulled.
He says: Some plants have thorns that point
in both directions, so if an animal gets tangled
the thorns catch, no matter which way it pulls.

Mathematician

Pythagoras knew
the beauty of silence
when he realized
mathematical order spreads
throughout the physical world;

that the cosmos,
from outermost galaxy
to individual atom
is filled with structure expressed
by mathematical terms.

But did he know the power
that exists with silence?
How power and beauty
take up the same position
in space?

If Pythagoras prayed
to find numbers
in squares and cubes
his focus only on shapes
and sounds, he may have discovered

the reason an apple falls from a tree.
Why the universe is subject to laws.
Why the power of prediction
and the taming of nature
would cause rapid disbelief.

If Pythagoras prayed,
the power in silence
would be beautiful;
his mind a landscape of coasts
and islands only he could see.

I Pray Near Honeybees

I pray near the honeybees.
Some stand guard
while others fan their wings
to keep the hive cool.

I close my eyes.
The honeycomb slopes;
the hive is dark.
Bees forage.

They move in circles and cross at angles.
They sense vibrations that lead to nectar.
One hopes for small circles.
Another is dizzy.

In the tree above, a robin sings.
Not for pleasure or to pass the time,
but to warn others
that it is dangerous to come.

I hear the bees
and realize the emotion of prayer
is the result of sharing.
That a play performed on a stage,
is better than reading it alone.

The Badger

I watch as the female badger
tries to take honey from worker bees.
Her nose is stung and she leaves the burrow
only to scoot back for a second go.
Her body is a hurricane the bees cannot hear.
When they sense her vibration, a swarm lands
on her fur to plant their stingers.
They are willing to die for their honey
and the badger leaves to recover outside.
Her need is relentless—she must have everything
honey, larvae, wax, and will spoil them all.
When she enters again the bees close their legs
to cover every part of their work.
But this time she uses her claws
and takes a piece of comb in her mouth
and another, and another.
The bees know her need like they know their own
and work to rebuild, but theirs
is a field of death and sweetness
as the badger sucks and sucks in the shade.

The Seizure

I told my dog to stop having the seizure
but it wasn't like telling her to sit or stay--
This time, her body wouldn't listen.
Instead, her eyes asked me to end this upset,
her weight an upheaval on the tile floor.
I watched her legs twitch
and her tongue hang to the left,
the saliva dripping out of her mouth
as urine flowed like a rivulet
unsure of direction or time.
When her teeth pressed against each other,
a focus of shape and groove,
I knew I couldn't control the spasms
stubborn and tight and
sealed off from human contact.
So I picked her up and put her in the car
and drove to the vet with one hand on the wheel
and the other on her abdomen.
I said: *Stay alive. You must stay alive.*
But her mind was off course,
stuck somewhere in the middle of death
roaming the halls of the afterlife,
discussing the politics of owner and master
with an Italian Greyhound,
as I focused on the road and the aim of my words:
The orders, the commands,
the stern tone of my voice, forgotten
in her place of discovery.

The Day We Put My Dog To Sleep

I listened to Iz's *over the rainbow* on repeat
and thought about the pet psychic.

The night before, while flipping channels
I found her doing a segment on owners who
wondered if they made the right decision.
The pet psychic said: You made the right decision. Maggie is here now.
And there's a man with her.

My father, the woman said.
Your father, and she's running
and she wants you to know that she thanks you for freeing her
that you did the right thing, because in the end
all she wanted was to be released from her body.

The day we put my dog to sleep
I yelled at my girlfriend for something she didn't do.
For something I can't remember.
I watched a movie.
The kind where you say this is so stupid
I can't believe I'm watching this.
I thought about eating the rest of the pretzels
but went on Ebay, looking for Smurf episodes.

I tried to print an auction, but the voice on the computer said
Alert, there is a problem with the printer, check the finder.
I checked the outlets instead, and found
leaning against the wall
a bag of pictures I'd forgotten about.
Pictures of Lucy chasing birds and tearing up stuffed animals.

I heard a buzzing sound
as the printer suddenly worked, printing the same page twice
and after, the voice from before:

Alert. Alert. The black ink cartridge is missing.
But when I looked, it was still there.
Simple. Black. Resting in its holder; clicked in, safe.

Echoes

I'm thinking of my mother
and how, before our neighbor died, she said
he wanted to be put in a mayonnaise jar
because he loved mayonnaise.

She didn't know where she wanted to be
but she wanted her body put inside of something--
This was important to her.

We sat in two chairs on the porch.
A lizard settled onto a flower.
That's the lip, she said, *the lip of the orchid that he's standing on.*

He swallowed, his throat a half glowing moon.
Why he?
To avoid *it*; to make it personal.
The lizard loves the flower, but the flower loves only herself.

And was it a lip?
No, it was a tongue
contrasting the pale sepals and dark petals--

A powerful red tongue
jutting out like the lizard's throat
an echo of each petal's pattern.

I mentioned icewine from Germany.
Canadian, she said, *never from Germany.*

From Okanagan Valley
in the peacock-blue bottle with the slim neck
the silver leaf and the silver stem--
Yes, and almost see through, she said.

My Father's Hands

There was a black belt that hung
next to a Harry Chapin picture
in his office that I was afraid of

but it was his hands, thick and calloused
that I was afraid of more and it was his voice
that made me jump.

He only pushed when I was fresh to her.
When I said *No* or *Yeah... But!*
He never did it unless there was a reason and

it wasn't like he flicked lit cigarettes on me
or caused bruises to appear on my body.
No, it wasn't like that. There was always a reason.

It stopped for years until I was eighteen
and drove into the garage, parking in a space
that was almost too small for my car.

He ran outside, said *You'll hit my car.*
Told me to get out, stuck his hand through
the rolled down window. When I said *No*

his face changed, the same way it did
before he slapped me when I was a child.
He tried to grab my neck but I moved

to the passenger seat, sticking my boots
in his face, kicking as hard as I could
spraining his wrist and breaking one of his fingers.

When he went to the hospital
she yelled at me. I told her about his hands
that I remembered holding them in the park

once in New York in the winter, when we went
sleigh riding down a hill and he sat behind me
keeping me steady, keeping me safe.

Wellwood Cemetery, Pinelawn, 1998

I took the Southern State Parkway to exit 35,
thinking, *I used to hold her arm when we went walking;*
thinking, *touching her made me feel so uncomfortable.*

I turned onto Wellwood Avenue and saw the cemetery on the right.
The overgrown plants and chain link fence
served as a divider from the road it was on.

I parked the car, walked into the office and said to the woman,
I'm here to see my grandmother's grave-- the Sussman-Picker Family Circle, please.
I left holding a map: I was to walk down Central Avenue,
past Daniel Road, past Ezra Road, and make a right
on Maccabee Road to South Avenue.
Rows of marked graves reminded me that I missed her death.
And the funeral.

The last time we spoke she was in the hospital
because she thought my aunt, who lived next door,
was poisoning her food.
She wandered eight miles from her house,
and told the stranger who found her
that she couldn't drive because my aunt cut the brakes in her car.

I called the hospital to see how she was.
She said, When are you having surgery to remove those breasts?
Your voice is so deep now.
Then she changed the subject,
saying my aunt poisoned the food in the cafeteria,
and that she was starving.

I walked through rows of graves
and found the spot where she was buried.
I remembered going shopping with her at Roosevelt Field.
She was saying, *Get what you want. It doesn't matter if they're for boys.*

Then we went to Woolworth's and sat at the counter
on red stools. I spun in circles while we waited
for rice pudding and tuna melts.

She said to the waitress, Is this coffee from the fresh pot?
I only drink coffee from the fresh pot.
I looked at her and she was smiling.
Then she was laughing.
Laughing out loud at death,
like it was Johnny Carson on the TV.

Your Nature

To see you again
will be different from any of our reunions.
Do you remember when we met?
I was one.
We began this way, doing young stuff.
You were so old, three,

and so so beautiful when you turned twelve,
that I wanted to kiss the inner part of your arm
and work my way up.

I think we were always tempted by each other.

Do you?
I mean
the way girls
are likely to kiss
to see if
they'd enjoy it.

I remember how you held me
when my dog
was left for dead on the highway
and how you
withdrew from me
when your dog Bosco died.

I was like pine
and you
were a snowfall—

sliding off a part of me your nature intended you to.

Dark Persistent Blue

I think of you
when I see
an evening moon
scattered leaves
in the ease of fall.
I study the curve
we make with distance.
I want to weave
through sky
in threads of folding stars
slip between layers
of the quilted patterns
and sew you
to the dark persistent blue.

For You

Orchids are my flower, too.
You sit next to me on the sand.
Your glasses are slipping.
You know exactly what I like.

We talk of goth clubs and cigarettes.
Of *Christian Death*,
and smoking meditation, and how
our place in the universe was close,

how we were born close,
that our mapped out worlds,
our mapped out words,
were enough so that one day
we'd meet unexpected,

agree to spend the day together,
almost twelve hours together,
to find we are as comfortable
as the stingrays we saw
but as alone as the sea turtle, too,
in his sweeping tides.

The Red

The words chosen are the same; milk, fire,
body, leaves; but we are not.
The moon, the shadows, the earth,

the snow haven't much in common
except that they're echoes of each other.

But are we?
The meeting was easy;
the time spent is not.

We talk about the color red-- flaming red,
alien red, air and canary red.

There are leaves the color of fire,
and a tree that watches over us
its base the shade of an overcast day.

The red is here, too; it's in the sky
trying to wash us in its graphic bath:
It says *We're not the meaning behind this repetition.*

It says *Just because we write villanelles
just because we write blue blue blue and
fire fire fire doesn't mean we belong together.*

Your Image In Watercolor

Your image in watercolor.
Not on silk or vellum, but on paper.

First, your face.
Your pale skin and red hair.
Then, your arms around my chest.
Now, my face.

Our heads touch.
I stand on the grass, nude.
You try to close yourself around me.
My lips are full.
My eyes are sad.

The tree wants you.
It wraps itself around you.
And around my thigh.

How beautiful you are now.
Your leaves finely toothed,
your fruit covered with silver.
You are wild,
your pink flowers longing for red.

We Have Sex

For the first time
my body is as familiar as the lines
on my right palm, the life line clearly defined,
the fate line just as obvious.

You are the first one who makes me feel like a man.
You are the first one who touches my chest,
plays with the curling hair.

You say, *I can feel it inside*,
and I believe you finally, after countless fights,
after accusing you of just saying that
to make me feel better.

I believe it's true,
that what I have to work with,
something no bigger than my thumb,
is better than what you've had in the past,

because when we finish
I realize that what's between my legs
isn't the only thing that defines me as male.

Because when we finish, out of breath and shaking,
you say, *Let's do it again*.

Bloodline

My name will not live on.
Does it matter?
People say bloodlines should continue,
but it's really the ego talking in your ear,
chattering like a gossip.
It whispers nonsense, tries to be important.

Why should I listen to such a thankless thing,
that grows in size until it's acknowledged?

The gene ends here, like a *do not enter* sign
that points to a dirt road.
At the end of the road, farmland.
Green fields, rows of sunflowers,
and behind that, a skeleton
of a burned down amusement park.

This is a dreamlike idea, that part of you
will continue to live,
somewhat surreal, somewhat real.
I don't care if my name lives,
if my bloodline continues.
I have to say this, otherwise I'd go mad.

Danny And The Pink Princess Phone

I took him to Toys R Us.
We walked down every aisle and looked at hundreds of toys.
He was four.
I'd been raising him for three years, by now I was used to the way
he carefully selected what he wanted, looking at the packaging,
studying the pictures, listening to any sounds the toy made.
We were in a section of the store specifically for girls now,
lots of pink, the color of ripe watermelon.
There was a toy phone in the clearance section,
the box crumpled and open.
I want this, daddy, he said, running over to it, picking it up,
pressing its buttons, blowing on the paper tassels
that were hanging from the plastic handle.
I stood motionless, hands at my sides
staring at the base that was covered in pink fur.
It looked like a madman scattered the fur in bright red glitter.
I supported his decision, but knew others wouldn't.
Later, we'd have a talk about boy toys and girl toys and why
it's okay to play with any kind of toy he wanted to.
You're my friend. Call me, I heard, after he pushed a number on the phone.
Next to the number, there was a picture of Snow White smiling,
her hair perfectly done, and next to her, Cinderella,
and next to her, Belle from Beauty and The Beast.
Next to each number, there was a princess.
Can I have this? Danny asked.
He held the phone under his arm.
I want them to be my girlfriends, he said.
When we got to the register, the cashier looked at me funny,
paused before taking the pink princess phone out of Danny's hands,
asked if we found everything okay.
I said yes, we found exactly what we wanted,
and no, we didn't need a bag, because he'll be opening it

and playing with it in the car.
But on the way out, Danny grabbed my hand
and frowned, said he changed his mind,
that he wanted the army truck and the army men, instead.
I pictured their intimidating faces, their green guns and hard stances.
It was a sad kind of relief, and I felt ashamed because of it,
as we walked back into the store to buy the army trucks and the army men,
their muscular plastic bodies pressing up against the plastic.

What We Heard

We sat in the cemetery under the enormous tree
and looked through its branches and leaves
past the dark sky, through a star and close to the moon.
We went away, lying on our backs
walked into a new space that held us close.
It took our hands and opened them up.
It looked at our palms, it made us forget
about the blanket and books, about the living below
about the haunted tree with its thick roots and decaying base.
It said *yes*.
It said *this is no coincidence, your work is important*.
We could have given up at any time and pulled away
running through the moon yelling Fire!
It was our decision as we listened to it say
you'll start your lives underwater but then flower above it.
We realized it is possible
despite the earthquakes below, despite the spreading flames
we agreed it is possible
to resemble the seasons, to survive above the snowline.
To be submissive to everything-- water, leaves, snow, flowers
even for just minutes-- then to be flooded by it all.

Where Bodies Don't Exist
   For Brandon Teena

I could hold your soul like a King's cup.
Mission bells on the hillside.
I could turn you to body; to man.

I saw their entry, and your blood.
I whispered *There will never be*
one language, as light turned
at the mixture of body and water.

I hummed to you in silence, and breath.
The breath you breathed into me I took,
your chapped heat a test of faith
as wet as a harvest that drowns.

I whispered again: *There will never*
be one language.
Your eyes falling like nations,
your lashes thick with peace.

My words swept your ears
passed the labyrinth, rushed by surface
and through canal, taking you to a place
where bodies don't exist, where torture in form
is like a hand stretched over the sea.

Your spirit as ancient as the earth,
your strength a sound revival in the fields.

The Way We Endured

"This ultimate repetition, this ultimate theatre,
gathers everything in a certain way;
and in another way, it destroys everything;
and in yet another way, it selects from everything."
                                    --- Gilles Deleuze

At first we emerged from rock
the undercurrents following seahorses—
the pull forcing us deeper and deeper out.

When the ocean was just a body
we swam for miles
taking the sun like we were made from it
traveling through formations that history changed
never stopping for air—
our mouths open like the sea.
We lived as an island does
our land as great as the winds that swept over us
their gusts carrying hints of sound and scent.
We mapped ourselves out—
paced the growth
until we spread across terrain
our expansion a fine geography.
We set our hands down, skins hot
and rubbed each other raw.
We became patches of dry soil
but as the seasons came, we grew
our green hides blinding to any animal that looked.
And when we curled ourselves into a garden
there was a bloom like no other
until our leaves became tired and we watched them
take their place on the dirt we founded each other on.

It was cold when our roots emerged
but the snow was an eden, taking us to a new feeling
able to give recess to the past endured.

Acknowledgments

Some of the poems in this collection have previously appeared in the following magazines, periodicals, and anthologies, whose publishers and editors I thank. On occasion, poems have been further revised, or titles changed, since their original publication:

The Avatar Review; "Lines From A Villanelle"

Bamboo Ridge; "Fourteen," "Live As A Boy," "An Extension Of," "The Day I Almost Lost Myself," "What Comes With An Attraction Between Cousins," "Under The Moon," "The Seizure," "At The Gynecologist's Office" and "At The Roller Rink"

Bend, Don't Shatter anthology; "The Girl In The Boy's Dressing Room" and "The Boy Girl Game"

Breadcrumbscabs; "I Remember a Time"

The Chaffin Journal; "Dark Persistent Blue"

Fireweed; "This Body"

Four AM Poetry Review; "How A Body Survives"

The Georgetown Review; "East Hampton, 1985"

Gertrude: A Journal of Voice and Vision; "When A Place Begins"

Ghoti; "Man Stands Three Times in Sydney"

Illuminations; "Her Taste"

The Pedestal Magazine; "Elderly Boy, Young Jew"

Poetica Magazine; "Among The Stones Of Fire"

Rain Bird; "The Badger"

The Rio Grande Review; "The Nature Of Insects"

Tinfish; "How A Body Survives"

Visions International; "Matchmaker"

About The Author

Jody Helfand has an MA in English and an MFA in Creative Writing, and lives and works in Hawaii. His work has appeared in over 50 journals, magazines, and anthologies, including *Visions International, The Pedestal Magazine, Fireweed, Bamboo Ridge, The Georgetown Review, The Rio Grand Review, Memorious, Illuminations* and others. He is currently working on his second book of poems about The Holocaust and his memoir about his gender change. He has hundreds of book recommendations, including *The Hours* by Michael Cunningham, *The Power of Your Subconscious Mind*, by Joseph Murphy, *The Wild Iris*, by Louise Gluck, and *Infinite Self* by Stuart Wilde. Some of his favorite places to visit are Cannon Beach, Stanley Park, and Vancouver Island. In his free time, he loves walking in nature, spending time with animals, lifting weights, going to concerts, traveling, reading, playing the drums, writing, and picking and eating fresh organic food. His dream is to own a house one day that has an ocean view in every room. His email address is jhrose22@hotmail.com and loves to correspond with other writers, so feel free to send him an email. Visit his website, too, at JodyHelfand.com for updates on readings, new projects and contests, and to read excerpts from his latest books.